How to Stop Procrastinating and Start Doing Now!

A Simple Guide to Overcome Procrastination,
Hacking Laziness and Taking Action
Through the Power of Self-Discipline

PERSONAL PRODUCTIVITY PROJECT

www.personalproductivityproject.com

Disclaimer

The follow eBook is reproduced below with the goal of providing information that is as accurate and reliable as possible. The authors of this book have made every attempt to ensure that the information provided in this book is verified. This book has been written for entertainment purposes. The views expressed within this book should not be taken as expert advice or consultation. However, the authors and publishers do not assume any responsibility for any omissions, errors or contrary interpretation of the subject matter herein. Please consult a professional prior to undertaking any of the actions endorsed within the book.

Adherence to all applicable laws and regulations, including international, federal, state and local governing professional licensing, business practices, advertising, and all other aspects of doing business in the US, Canada, or any other jurisdiction is the sole responsibility of the purchaser or reader. Neither the publishers nor the authors assume any liability or responsibility in any way for the actions of the reader. The reader assumes any and all responsibility of any actions they undertake as a result. Any perceived slight of any individual or organization is purely unintentional.

Your Free Gift

As a way of saying thanks for your purchase, we are offering a free report that's exclusive to readers of How to Stop Procrastinating and Start Doing Now!

Follow this link to grab your copy and subscribe our newsletter!

www.personalproductivityproject.com/free-gift

Table of Contents

Introduction

Congratulations! You've just made a decision that is about to change the course of your life. Unlike many procrastinators, you have already realized that you need to change and have taken the first step. Thank you for *Stop Procrastinating, Start Doing Now!* and we hope that you will find all the information within most beneficial to you.

Many procrastinators suffer from a similar fate. Perhaps you have a dream that has never been realized, or the stress of always waiting to the last moment is starting to wear you down. Maybe you have suffered socially or professionally due to your tendency to procrastinate. Whatever your situation, if you have recognized the need for change, then we have good news for you – you have come to the right place. This book is designed to provide a lasting solution to your procrastination problem.

There are three parts. Part one defines what procrastination is, the different forms it takes (many of which are not often recognized as procrastination), consequences that procrastination brings into our lives, and what is going on in our minds when we procrastinate. Knowing what goes on when we procrastinate will be useful to understand what causes the problem and understand why the things you've tried have not worked.

Part two discusses three commonly utilized options for overcoming procrastination. It discusses which of these works, and why.

Part three contains some steps that will be useful to you after starting to take action. They will help you improve your productivity right from the start. Instead of wondering where to begin with your new-found knowledge, you will have four short steps to action and efficiency. You will be amazed at how these tools will start you on a life-changing journey.

Experience has shown that the tools are useful only after the job has been set up. It is no coincidence that those who focus on the instruments instead of the dynamics of procrastination have never stopped procrastinating or have fallen back into old habits. People must start the work before picking up the tools.

One last thing. Since one of the strategies procrastinators use to delay is to endlessly research and seek information, this book is specifically designed to be a quick read. So, you are only a couple of hours from the end of procrastination and the beginning of the action!

Part I

CHAPTER 1:

Understanding Procrastination

What It Is, Why We Do It and the Many Forms It Can Take in Our Lives

I sit down at my desk and set out to answer a dozen unpleasant emails that I have been avoiding. I do not enjoy confrontation so I am filled with dread. A notification pops up on Facebook, and I think to myself, 'I deserve a break. I'll just peek for five minutes.' At the end of five minutes, I say to myself, "Five minutes more" and suddenly I have spent two hours scrolling through my newsfeed and clicking through puppy pictures. What happened? Procrastination. Procrastination happened.

Procrastination is an irrational decision to delay doing something. Why is it irrational? Because even though we know we know what we *should be doing,* we choose to purposely postpone or delay it. Or we may even choose to do something else, thereby procrastinating. If we look at most forms of procrastination closely, we will realize that it is a choice for instant gratification over future reward or suffering. In the Facebook example, I have made an irrational choice to do something useless but pleasurable instead of doing something less pleasant but of much greater value. I don't want to do the necessary task of writing the emails, because it isn't pleasant or it is not something I like to do. Therefore, I choose to linger by either postponing it, or doing other tasks which are less demanding (or more rewarding) right now. In this scenario, there is one very important thing that you need to take note of – *procrastination is a very short-term vision. By procrastinating, you're losing sight or not seeing the bigger picture (medium-long term vision) which reminds you why you should be doing the task you're currently choosing to procrastinate.*

Productivity sacrificed various social media posts or distractions isn't the only manifestation of procrastination. Procrastination can manifest as laziness, i.e. "I'll go to the gym tomorrow." It can appear as disorganization. "I don't want to file those papers now, it can wait." Poor productivity is another manifestation of procrastination. The unproductive person thinks, "That can wait until tomorrow," but tomorrow never comes. Or procrastination can even appear as a general lack of motivation and a fatalistic approach to life. "I would love to be start my own business, but it would never work out."

Different Types of Procrastinators

Just as there are many forms of procrastination there are many types of procrastinator. Here is a look at some of the most common types of procrastinator:

The Delayer

This is probably the most obvious type of procrastinator. This person doesn't want to something so he or she keeps putting it off into the future. The Delayer's motto is "why do today what you can put off until tomorrow." The Delayer comes across as lazy as he or she is not particularly good at getting things done.

The Day Dreamer

The Day Dreamer takes pleasure in musing about the 'big picture things of life' and is bored by the humdrum details of daily tasks. Rather than focus on the necessary and unpleasant evils of life such as a looming work deadline, he or she prefers to remain wrapped up in their (much more pleasurable) fantasy world.

The Justifier

The Justifier avoids one task by accomplishing a different task. This procrastinator might avoid doing a homework project by organizing the messy shoe closet. The Justifier deflects what he didn't do by focusing on a smaller and more trivial project that he can easily accomplish.

The Adrenaline Junkie

The Adrenaline Junkie thrives on the "thrill" of leaving a task to the last minute. They feel that they work their best under the intense pressure of a deadline. This type of procrastinator may be easily bored and therefore seeks ways to make unpleasant tasks more exciting.

The Worrier

Thoughts of failure induce anxiety in the Worrier. They prefer not to do something because it seems either unnecessary or too much of a risk. Negative emotions overwhelm them and they prefer to remain in their comfort zone and do nothing. This procrastinator has low self-esteem and doubts whether they can succeed. Rather than attempt something and risk the pain of failure, they remain inactive because they believe this is the must safer option. They think they are saving themselves from the hurt and disappointment that possible failure may bring.

The Planner

The Planner thrives on making list and derives a sense of satisfaction from making perfect plans. Unfortunately for the Planner, making the plans is easier and more satisfying than the effort it takes to finish the task. Ultimately the lists are just another excuse to avoid completing the task for which the planner is planning.

The Overloaded Circuit

The Overloaded Circuit is weighed down by a variety of worries, responsibilities and other cares that haunts him or her from every corner of life. This person is like an electrical circuit with too many cords plugged in. Due to stress, too much mental energy is going out and the procrastinator hovers close to burnout. This person attempts to avoid additional stress by pushing tasks off to a later date and may waste time by seeking stress relieving activities like binge watching television or surfing the internet.

Whatever type of procrastinator you are, there is the same root cause. The moment it comes time for you to take some action, the (irrational) part of you that wants to please (or to avoid pain) wins. The rational part of your brain that sees the benefit of a future reward is no longer in control.

In the 1960s a scientist named Walter Mischel studied this phenomenon of instant gratification. He began a series of experiments that is now widely referred as the Marshmallow Experiment. He was exploring the ability of children to delay gratification for future reward. In this experiment, a group of preschoolers was shown two plates with varying quantities of marshmallows or other snacks, a small snack and a larger snack. When the experimenter left the room, they could ring the bell immediately, thus ending the experiment, and eat the smaller snack or they could wait 15 minutes and receive the larger reward. It was an experiment to see how these children did when given a choice of instant gratification or larger future reward.

What is interesting about this experiment, is that a follow-up experiment was also done on some of the participants when they reached middle age. Those children who were better at delaying gratification for future reward had achieved higher test scores, reported greater self-esteem, and were even in better general health than those who were tempted by instant gratification.

We all know what procrastination is and that it is detrimental to our overall well-being and success but why do we do it?

Future Self and Present Self

As we have seen instant gratification or pleasure seeking, is at the root of procrastination. Imagine that in your brain is a pilot at the helm of an aircraft attempting to safely steer you towards your destination. Behavioral scientists would call this pilot your "Future Self."

As future self dutifully flies along, charting a tidy course to your destination a monkey jumps into the cockpit, twisting knobs, pulling levers and causing mayhem and damage to the craft. This would be called this your "present self." Behavioral Science research says that these two "selves" comprise your decision making and are at odds with each other. Only future self (the pilot) can forgo distraction and the fun of instant gratification in order to achieve a long-term goal. Present self is all about pleasure in the moment, however, and unfortunately tends to control of our decision making. This monkey-in-the cockpit scenario is what happens when we procrastinate and it is what behavioral science calls time-inconsistency.

At its core time-inconsistency is the idea that human beings think too much about their present selves and too little about their future self. For example, if I think about my fitness goals a year from now, of course I want to be thinner, stronger and more athletic. This is me in "future self" mode. If I am simply thinking and planning for the future, my future self can be considered. But if someone offers me a donut I will most likely eat it. When given the option for immediate pleasure, "present self" takes over.

This is because behaviorally we skew towards making decisions that give us the most immediate benefit or reward rather than exercise patience and put in the hard work for the possibility of an even bigger reward. This is especially true if the consequences are in the distant future.

The person who scrolls Facebook instead of starting a project and the person who endlessly daydreams are not that different. The internet surfer receives momentary pleasure by reading his or her newsfeed. The dreamer continuously thinks about grand things from the comfort of their present life never risking the pain of failure or the effort of trying. In both examples a pleasure-seeking "monkey" (or perhaps a pain-avoiding one) seeks the most comfortable choice in the short-term, largely ignoring how it will affect their future selves. This is at the heart of almost all procrastination.

CHAPTER 2:

Building Unhappiness

How Procrastination Can Ruin Your Life

We have just discussed the many forms that procrastination can take in our lives. But have you ever thought about the damage that procrastination can do to your career, relationships, well-being and even health? You might be aware that procrastination is not good for you, but you might not realize the extent of the damage that procrastination can cause. If we are aware of all the ways procrastination negatively impacts us, we can start to confront this issue in all areas of our lives.

Procrastination and the Quality of Life

If you are a chronic procrastinator, one thing you will know is that the procrastination habit can really sap the joy out of your life. Here's an example of a scenario. There's a college student who has an honors thesis due in the Spring of their college year. The student had nine months to research and craft a 20-50 page scholarly work on a topic related to their major. From the outside, that seemed all too easy to accomplish. The student would only have to write a page per week! However, there is one thing the student forgot to take into account – other assignments, and the tendency to procrastinate.

Fast forward to the week it was due. That week began finals week of the semester with the paper less than halfway finished. The student ended the week with an 18 page (!) paper and had slept a total of maybe 8 hours in 5 days. To this day, the student feels the relief of being done with that paper. The stress of rushing to meet the deadline, trying to finish the paper in the hurry resulted in the student producing work which was far below what was expected of them. The student did get a passing grade, but deep down, knew that they could have done so much better if only the student hadn't procrastinated.

The student was sick, miserable and filled with guilt by the time the paper was finally handed in. Miserable knowing that the days spent leading up to the deadline were not fully utilized, and filled with guilt knowing this could have gone better. Guilt knowing 100% effort was not given.

Procrastination and Relationships

Procrastination can harm both professional and personal relationships in a variety of ways. The most obvious way that procrastination can harm relationships is through the damage it does to our reputation and the way that others perceive us. Professionally, this can be greatly damaging. If you can only be productive in a panic at the last moment you may be viewed as disorganized, unreliable, and irresponsible. You may be viewed as incompetent or ill-suited to your work. This in turn can affect your ability to achieve your professional goals and excel in your career.

Another big way that procrastination damages all kinds of relationships is caused by stress that is a side effect of procrastination. When you procrastinate, your mood can plummet and irritability increase. You can become a whirlwind of negative nervous energy. This by itself can cause tension between friends, teammates or lovers.

When procrastinators panic in the face of the looming deadline, the task at hand can become all-consuming.

Dates may be cancelled, promises broken and the procrastinator may become so absorbed in a project that he or she becomes distant. These things break trust and build resentment. An other-wise stable relationship can crack under the weight of chronic procrastination.

Some procrastinators, those who procrastinate due to low self-esteem and self-doubt may actually be relationship saboteurs. This type may succeed at beginning a relationship, as things become more serious, though, they can begin to sabotage it, even without consciously choosing to do so. It comes back to the same issue of fear of failure and wanting to protect oneself from a painful and unknown future. It is a classic defense mechanism where the side effects affect the following aspects:

- **Procrastination and Health**

    Another insidious side effect of chronic procrastination is the ways in which it can damage one's health. Once again, the stress that accompanies procrastination is a major culprit here. While people procrastinate to avoid stress and difficulty, they actually prolong the amount of time that they experience stress. And when they operate under pressure at the last minute, this further amplifies the stress they put themselves under. Stress, as we all know, is a contributing factor to a wide array of health concerns.

Procrastinators of the avoidance variety also tend to put off their own routine health maintenance. Not only does their procrastination cause them undue stress, but it further damages their health by letting small health issues become bigger ones. This could be delaying a doctor's appointment until one is more seriously ill, or it could be avoiding diet and exercise until one has acquired the diseases associated with a sedentary lifestyle and a poor diet. The procrastinator may end up experiencing a synergistic effect of their behaviors on their well-being. Procrastination causes stress, and causes the procrastinator to avoid treatment, both of which lead to poor health, which cause more stress, and so on.

- **Procrastination and the Lazy Lifestyle**

  We live in a world today that is designed for convenience. Everything is much easier these days, often as simple as a few quick taps on our smart devices to get the job done without us ever having to leave our homes. Our lifestyle choices could be feeding into our procrastination tendencies, because of the lazy lifestyle it is encouraging us to lead. Which is why a procrastinator has to pay attention to the choices that they make? Are these choices encouraging laziness instead of productivity? One example of this phenomenon is the convenience of fast food and takeaway outlets that are aplenty. When you've had a long day, it is tempting to reach for the easier option of buying a meal instead of cooking on your own. Eventually, the effects of poor dieting and a lack of proper nutrition could potentially cause weight gain and a depletion of energy which comes full cycle. This then encourages even lazier tendencies. The more that you feel you don't have the energy for something, the easier it is to give in to quicker, faster, easier and lazier options, even if they result in a poorer lifestyle overall.

- **The Greatest Danger of Procrastination**

When some people talk about their procrastination, they may say that procrastination helps the get things done. It motivates them in to swift action. They may even be able to recall a time where they raced to the deadline in an almost-heroic fashion. You may or may not relate to this sort of procrastination bravado, but what do people mean when people say that procrastination helps them? Going back to the monkey-in-the cockpit illustration from the previous chapter, people who succeed in spite of their procrastination do so because a third character enters the scene. Usually in the case of procrastination, the pilot (your decision-making future self) is flying along, and the monkey (pleasure seeking current self) enters the scene and starts to distract the pilot and take him off course. But then, another animal slithers in. We'll call this animal the "panic python". The panic python is the natural predator of the fun-loving monkey, and quickly chase s him off.

You are probably all too familiar with this python. He is the panic that showed up in college when you had a paper due in the morning and only two sentences on the page. He tends to show up any time there is a deadline dangerously looming and the task is nowhere near completion. Procrastinators who seem to think that their procrastination benefits them, tend to think of situations in which there is a deadline to startle them back to reality and productivity. Their procrastination is finite. But what happens when there is no deadline?

Without the urgency of a deadline to throttle you into action, you are stuck in an endless holding pattern of procrastination. This is the most insidious kind of procrastination; the kind that can ruin the life of the procrastinator. It is the kind that is so subtle that a person may not even realize that it is happening. It can happen over weeks, months and even years as a person puts off what he or she deems to hard or too uncomfortable to do and instead fills his or her life with what is easy, comfortable and pleasurable in the moment. Life can pass the procrastinator by and so many hopes, dreams and plans are never realized. The procrastinator is filled with guilt and self-loathing in reflective moments. What this all adds up to is a wasted life filled with discontentment and unhappiness.

Laziness – It Hinders Success

Being lazy can do real damage in your efforts towards success. Everyone wants success, there is no one that is going to tell you they do not want to be successful in life. Everyone desires success, the difference between the ones who achieve success and the ones who fail is the amount of effort to put into achieving that success. Procrastinating and being lazy will never get you far, it is a hindrance and it stops you from achieving the success that you should:

- **Laziness Makes Others Perceive You Negatively –** Laziness is associated as something negative. These negative connotations are hard for anyone to look past, and if you are associated with laziness, it can be very difficult for you to convince people why they should work with you. If you want to achieve success, laziness is the one word you need to stay well away from and never give anyone the opportunity to associate you with that word.

- **Laziness Affects Your Credibility -** Your reputation is one of your most valuable traits you could have, and the minute people don't have any faith in you is the minute your chances of success fade further away. A bad impression is one that is hard to erase. Think about this scenario for a minute: would you want to work with someone who comes off as lazy? Or shows any signs of lazy tendencies and habits? It is unlikely the answer is going to be a resounding YES. Being lazy isn't just going to stop you from getting things done well, but it will also have a serious impact on your credibility and your reputation among your peers and the people with whom you work with.

- **Laziness Makes You a Liability at Work** - There is no employer that is going to look at a lazy person and say this person is of value to my company. Ever. There is NO employer anywhere in this world who is going to make hiring a lazy person who procrastinates one of their top priorities. Put yourself in the employer's shoes. If you were running a company of your own, you wouldn't want to employ a lazy person either because they are a liability. No company is going to waste good resources on an employee who doesn't perform at their best, when they can easily find another employee who will, and that is how being lazy puts your job at serious risks if you're not careful about it.

- **Laziness Hinders Your Progress and Your Success -** Working towards success is an on-going effort, because you need to continuously grow and work until you have reached your goal. Working to overcome procrastination and laziness is just as hard. Laziness will leave you stagnant and never experiencing the growth potential that you should. A lazy mindset will immediately shy away and retreat from any responsibility the minute there are signs that too much work or effort is going to be involved in getting things done.

- **Laziness Exhausts and Diminishes Your Mental Powers -** Our brains are just like every other muscle in our body. If we don't use it, eventually it will start to deteriorate. If your life is dominated by procrastination and lazy tendencies, it is a life that has no real use for proper brainpower. Over time a lazy person's brain will not function as well as a someone who is hardworking for example. The less you utilize it, the more your memory power will weaken over time.

If you are reading this book, then you have already realized that procrastination is a problem in your life. Reading this chapter may have given you an "aha" moment where you realized how procrastination was affecting you more than you realized. Now that you are armed with even more reasons to confront this issue, let's begin look at how to overcome it!

Part II

CHAPTER 3:

Motivation – More Than a Feeling?

Why Motivation Doesn't Work to Overcome Procrastination

Where Many People Start

Many people, when asking themselves how to stop procrastination, will look first to motivation to help them overcome the vicious cycle. This is because people generally feel that the motivation is what fuels this action in the beginning. Think of it as a three-way process:

thoughts (motivation) => positive emotional state => action

A person wanting to get fit in the gym might plaster their walls and refrigerator with pictures of in-shape people for motivation's sake. Someone wanting to succeed in business might listen to a motivational speech on self-confidence and achievement. Instinctively, this seems like a good place to start. The modern world even has a whole slew of speakers and writers whose careers are dedicated to motivating us. It is a lucrative business. But it is one that is built on a lie, or at least a half-truth. Motivation, on its own, accomplishes nothing. Why?

Here's an example to illustrate and explore why motivation is not a cure for procrastination. Let's say that you want to lose 10 pounds after watching the scale slowly creep up on you. You then inspire yourself to act. You think to yourself: "Today is the day I start cutting calories. I'm really going to do it this time." You recall how good it felt last time you were physically fit, and you promise yourself that your memories of this proud accomplishment are going to carry you to the proverbial finish line.

Each morning, you start to psych yourself up, saying, 'I am really going to do follow my diet today.' You read motivational blogs on the subject. This helps you stay on track with your diet for a while. You see small victories on the scale and that further excites you and renews your motivation. One day, though, you get a reprimand from your boss at work. Your mood tanks and you decide to self-medicate with cookies and a Netflix binge. This makes you feel bad about cheating on your diet and so you think, 'Why bother? I have messed everything up anyway, there is no point in evening trying'. Your motivation fails and the diet is over.

Procrastination and the Negative Mind

Being negative is always the easier option, being positive requires a lot more effort put into it. Having a negative state of mind will only feed into your reasons to procrastinate, because you'll always be able to find a hundred reasons not to do something, even though you may have one good reason why you should.

If you don't give yourself enough credit and believe in yourself enough, you will never find the extra push and the drive you need to break the cycle of procrastination. Sometimes a negative mindset can cause you to start believing that you're not good enough, or you're not deserving enough and thus, it would be better to just not do it at all rather than to try and risk failure.

Why Motivation Doesn't Work

Why doesn't motivation work to overcome procrastination? Simple. Motivation is based on human emotions and human emotions, like people themselves, are highly changeable and susceptible to a plethora of outside forces. Motivation is not a dependable bedrock to build your house upon. It is more like sand on the beach, changing with every tide.

This is the same reason that the gym is so crowded in January, but back to normal by mid-February. People are carried along by the emotional high of a New Year's resolution. They say to themselves, 'This is a new year, and I am going to be a new me.' They feel proud of their resolve, and their short-term accomplishments spur them on for a month or so. Then life happens. The "high" of the New Year fades and with it, the positive emotions that were carrying them along. When the emotional tide wanes, so does their ability to stick it out in the gym.

Laziness –A motivation Rut

Just as motivation pushes us up, the lack of motivation (demotivation) leads us into a downward spiral. Or, to put it more plainly, causes us to descend into laziness.

If you are someone who believes the lie that you must *feel* motivated in order to act, you are especially susceptible to this danger. This is because laziness is

simply a lack of motivation that has becomes habitual. In order to understand this phenomenon, let's
go back to the diet example and the downward spiral of demotivation. The demotivation-spiral happens when an emotional crisis robs us of our *feeling*
of motivation. Your boss yells at you, and interrupts
the emotional high of your diet success. As motivation wanes, you eat to comfort myself. Then you feel
guilty for cheating, and your motivation completely
dries up.

You start to think, *"if I fail at my diet once, that is not
such a big deal"*. But what tends to happen to someone
relying on motivation, is that after a few of these inevitable downward spirals, a person can become fatalistic in their thinking. *"Why should I even try to diet?"*
they may think: *"It never works. I always fail."* Their
self-esteem is damaged. The demotivation has become routine for this individual.

In other words, if we wait for motivation, we become
inert, and lazy. This leads to boredom, depression, and
low self-esteem. In such a state, motivation, with its
ties to our emotions, never show up. This forms a cycle where we wait for motivation, no motivation ap-
pears, and so we do not act. Inaction makes us feel bad

about our own laziness and these bad feelings make it even less likely that we can summon motivation. We are now in a habitual state of inaction and laziness.

Laziness goes by many names. Some would call it idleness, some call it slothfulness, indolence, lethargy and many more. It is a very dangerous habit to hold because it can quickly become a behavioral pattern if you indulge in it far too often. Here's the thing about laziness - it quietly creeps in and takes a hold of you and you won't even realize it until it's too late and it becomes hard to break out of that pattern of behavior. It is a vice that takes over without you even being aware of it, and that is what makes it dangerous. This is why you fall victim more often than you would like to procrastination.

It always starts out innocently enough, where you indulge in a couple of lazy days

because you feel you have earned this much-needed downtime. A person who acts only when they have the *feeling* to do so (or in other words, only when they feel motivated), slowly builds up a habit of becoming lazy. When you *feel* like doing something, only then will you do it. If you don't, you just wouldn't bother.

Because being lazy, relaxing and doing nothing can feel so good, you gradually start indulging in it more. You slowly begin to succumb to the idea and give in to your desires each time you feel you don't want to do something, until over time this pattern becomes a part of your lifestyle. It may seem harmless enough but overcoming laziness when it has fully set in is not as easy as it may seem.

Motivation Follows Action

Ask yourself these questions:

- Do I *feel* motivated to write a 30-page paper when I am staring at a blank computer screen?

- Do I *feel* like mastering a new language when I can barely stutter 'oui' and 'non'?

- Do I *feel* like running 100 miles as a warm up my cold muscles in the first 100 meters?

More than likely, you answered 'no' to the above questions. For the paper example, after researching and banging out a few paragraphs, the writer feels more comfortable and confident. This is when he begins to feel motivation on a project.

The language learner feels motivation as she learns a few more words and successfully stings together a few phrases.

The runner feels motivation rise with each passing mile.

Another quirk of motivation is that is often follows. When action is taken, small victories spark motivation, such as the language learner speaking a few phrases or the runner putting a few miles behind him. As the writer gains knowledge on the subject she gains confidence and motivation follows. This is the right three-way process:

Action => positive emotional state => motivation

Motivation's Rightful Place

So, is motivation a bad thing? Of course not. Motivation may start you in the right direction or show up once you have already begun to act. It can even help you accomplish smaller, short-term goals. When we understand how motivation works, we can use it to our advantage.

In order to master motivation, we must remember that it is based in our emotions. We can take advantage of positive emotional states or outside motivational factors to get us started on small projects. The positive emotions that accompany setting a New Year's resolution might be enough to get us started at the gym if we look to other strategies to keep us on the right path. The thought of an upcoming visit from your in-laws may be enough motivation to get you to clean out the shoe closet.

We can also remember that motivation often shows up late to the party. We can remind ourselves that even if we don't feel motivated now, we may get a needed boost of motivation once we get going.

However, at best, motivation is an unreliable friend. At worst it is a lie that can trap us in a holding pattern of laziness and inaction. For the long-haul we need something more dependable, something that is present when motivation is nowhere to be found.

CHAPTER 4:

Life Is a Marathon, Not a Sprint

Why Willpower Is Helpful, But Not an Ultimate Solution

Once people start to realize what happens when motivation fails because it is not under their control, they turn their attention to something that they know they *can* control – *willpower*. Merriam Webster dictionary defines willpower as energetic determination. Willpower is what helps us get out of bed in the morning and go to work, even though that is not a place most of us want to be. Nobody wants to spend 8 hours of their day cooped up in a cubicle doing a job they're not passionate about, but they do it anyway because they *know that they have to do.*

Will Power- A Closer Look

Scientifically, there is a specific part of our brain called the prefrontal cortex that controls our decision making, our ability to plan for the future, and make choices that benefit us in the long run. This part of the brain is located in the front of the skull behind the eyes. Studies have mapped the brains of those with weak and strong will power and have seen actual differences in activity of this area of the brain. This little section of the brain could be thought of the 'willpower muscle.' And it operates in much the same way that your other muscles do: if you do not use it you lose it! The good news is that, like muscle, it can be rebuilt, re-trained and strengthened.

Training the Willpower Muscle – Start Small and Build

If willpower is essentially a muscle, the only way to get more of it is to train over time. As we take small steps to go against our natural inclinations, we can slowly build up our willpower. If you struggle with writing academic papers, you could start small. Practice writing a page at a time, despite your feelings. Then two pages, then three.

If you struggle with making healthy food choices you could, by sheer force of will, eat one healthy meal a day, and work your way up to two, then three. You get the idea. As you train your willpower on these smaller tasks, it will become strong enough to tackle bigger and more complex challenges.

If you aren't sure where to being building up your willpower muscle, or if you realize that you have naturally weak willpower, a good place to start is by taking up a sport or going to the gym. The mind/ body connection is a powerful one and training them together can have a synergistic effect. If you begin at the gym by walking a half mile, then a mile, then jogging a little while, then running a 5 k, you will see a progress in your physical strength as well as the strength of your willpower.

Remember the adage, 'A journey of a thousand miles begins with a single step.' Think of tasks that you struggle with regularly and break them down into smaller chunks. Practice flexing your willpower muscles by achieving one small chunk of a task. As we discussed in previous chapters, motivation will often follow these small steps to action and help carry you along.

Willpower: Is it Really The Solution?

Willpower is beginning to look like the ultimate solution to our procrastination problem. It is something you can train up, unlike your emotions you can control it, so there is no downside, right? Think about this scenario:

In the morning, your alarm clock goes off. Your brain says "*Just 5 more minutes of sleep.*" Exerting your willpower, you counter with, "*I MUST get up and go to work. I WILL do it.*" You begrudgingly get out of bed and go to eat breakfast, where you are faced with a choice. Pastry or oatmeal? Again, you will yourself to make the healthy choice. "*I NEED to eat better. I promised myself I would. Don't even think about it that chocolate donut!*" You eat the oatmeal, resenting each bite. In the first ten minutes of your day you have already engaged in two battles of the will. It's going to be a long day.

Just imagining this scenario is enough to make one weary. There is a reason why. It takes a great deal of energy to go against our natural inclinations and exercise the power of our will. In the last decade or so, scientists started studying willpower and the idea that willpower is a limited resource. Scientist exploring this idea refer to it as willpower depletion.

One such study conducted by psychologist Roy Baumeister in 1996 tested the concept of willpower through what was called the Chocolate-and-Radish

Experience. In this experiment, Baumeister enticed a group of test subjects with the scent of freshly baked cookies. They were then led into a room with a plate of cookies and a bowl of radishes. Some test subjects were asked to eat the radishes while others were allowed to eat cookies. Afterwards, both groups were then given a complex geometry problem to solve. The group that ate radishes gave up on the math problem twice as fast as the group that ate cookies. The scientists behind this experiment concluded that the subjects who ate radishes depleted their reserves of willpower in resisting the cookie aroma. When they attempted the math problem, they simply had less willpower left that the group who got to eat cookies.

The big problem with wanting to use willpower to win the procrastination battle is that if you're going to spend your life fighting against your procrastination tendencies, just like in a real battle, it is only a matter of time before you tire out and fatigue. Because of this, very few people manage to successfully overcome procrastination through sheer willpower alone.

Good for the Sprint but not the Marathon

The good news is we can increase our willpower by intentional training. The bad news is that no matter rigorously we train, we will always have a finite amount of willpower and we may not be able to control when we run out of "gas." But when willpower sputters out, we will begin falling back into old procrastination habits. Still, willpower is an essential piece of the puzzle. In the last mile of a marathon, willpower will get you to the finish line. But what is going to get you to run the first twenty-five miles?

CHAPTER 5:

Overcoming Procrastination

What Self-Discipline Is and Why It Works

Our emotions are a volatile source, which makes them unreliable. Motivation relies on emotions which is why they don't always succeed. Willpower replies on grit and determination, which can be emotionally and physically exhausting and draining. This is where a *third* solution to the procrastination problem comes into play. A third solution which we *can* control and doesn't cost any extra energy – *self-discipline*.

Self-discipline is the ability to control yourself and to make yourself work hard or behave in a particular way without needing anyone else to tell you what to do. You don't even need anyone else to tell you what to think. Self-discipline seems very similar to willpower, but there are important differences: if willpower is the ability to find extra energy, self-discipline is the ability to take (and hold) the control of oneself and one's own thoughts. When you get a picture of discipline in action, it's quiet, it's determination to reach a goal, it's solid and grounded. There is no feeling of conflict and struggle. Self-discipline uses self-awareness and takes control of both mind and emotion to neutralize inner conflict and allow us to calmly progress towards our goals.

People Who Are Happier Are Those with High Levels of Self-Control

Did you know that the happiest people out there are the ones with the greatest self-control? Well, at least, according to a 2013 study by Wilhelm Hoffman it is. What Hoffman discovered in his study was that these individuals with greater self-control were far happier in life because they knew how to overcome conflicts which prevented them from achieving their goals. These high self-control individuals didn't spend a lot of time, energy or thought on actions which were going to be detrimental to their progress and health. These individuals had such high levels of self-discipline and control that their impulses and feelings were not the driving force of their decisions. These self-discipline and self-control qualities were exactly what allowed them to make decisions and choices which were rational, informed and well thought out to minimize the stress and anxiety they felt over it.

Just One Word

How do we begin to practice self-discipline? With a word that we know very well: "NO". Learning to say no to your thoughts means learning to choose which thoughts to welcome into your mind, and which ones to let go of without giving it much importance. We cannot choose what our next thoughts will be. However, what you *can do is learn to select and keep* the thoughts which are going to prove useful towards helping you achieve your goal. In this case, the goal is to overcome procrastination.

When you learn to say no to your own thoughts, you harness a powerful force: you become able to neutralize and remove harmful voices in your head. And in doing so, you create a space in your mind for *useful* thoughts. What might this look like? Let's say that you go to start a project and your mind is telling you *'just five more minutes of T.V.'*. If you acknowledge the voice telling you to procrastinate, you can consciously say 'no,' and move forward into action. You don't use emotion to motivate, or willpower to force yourself into action, to make a conscious decision to disagree with the thoughts telling you to procrastinate.

We have to avoid fighting the thoughts that tell us "*not yet*", "*still 5 minutes*", "*do it after*", etc. We have to learn simply say "*No*" and let go of the thought. Such thoughts must not be allowed to take root in our minds. Once again, imagine that alarm clock going off in the morning. That voice in your head still says "*Five more minutes of sleep.*" Instead of saying "*I WILL get up, I MUST*", you simply say "*no thanks*", and get out of bed. You head down to breakfast and there are no pastries to tempt you, because you already said "*No thanks*" to them at the grocery store.

A 'just say no' is a simple approach, but like our will-power muscles, there is some training that goes into it. It is a matter of retraining the brain and reframing our own thoughts in order to take control of them. Like our muscles of willpower, even for self-discipline there are workouts. It is about learning to recognize thoughts (not to force control) and to select which ones to let in and which ones to keep out of.

Using the Power of NO

There comes a point in everyone's life where you simply must put your foot down and say *no*. More importantly, you need to *mean it*.

The word "no" certainly has negative connotations associated with it, but in this context, it is going to be used as a tool that is going to help you establish a barrier that protects yourself and your interests first. By saying no, you are acknowledging what you will and will not put up with. You need to learn to say no, in order to say yes to bigger and better things. If a task or favor is going to deflect you away from your goals and cause you to procrastinate, this is an example of when you should be saying no.

Saying no may be a concept that you struggle with, and that's okay. A lot of people do. The feeling of guilt, not wanting to be the "bad guy" that has to say no is not a situation anyone wants to find themselves in. It will be uncomfortable and hard in the beginning, but as you slowly start to lose the urge to procrastinate, your momentum begins to build up towards achieving your goals. Saying no eventually becomes easier along the way. When you see yourself getting one step further towards achieving what you set your mind to, your inner strength, resilience and determination starts to shine through, and saying no then becomes something you *have to do* because you want to run past the finish line so badly. The closer you get to the finish line, the more determined you become to get there.

How do you know when to say no?

CHAPTER 6:

The "Happiness Formula"

and the Need for Self-Awareness

You can only know when to say no, when you know when to say yes. In other words, you need to know what you want in order to know what you don't want to do. For this, you must be self-aware. There is a great strategy to achieve this self-awareness: the happiness formula.

When you bear the burden of your duties, it can be very difficult to act, because nobody likes feeling obliged to do something that he has not chosen to do. The Formula of Happiness was created to remove this weight: when the duties become not only choices, but the best choices that can be made in that situation and at that time, to taking becomes the best solution.

The Happiness Formula

The happiness formula is a simple but very effective tool to always make informed choices.

It is a sequence of questions to ask yourself before taking an action:

1) Write down a task you must do. For example, I MUST write this-20-page report for my boss.

2) Turn the "I MUST" statement into a question that starts with "I WANT". For example: "*Do I want to write this 20-page report for my boss?*"

3) If the answer is YES, DO IT!

4) If the answer is NO ask to yourself: "*Am I willing to pay the consequences of leaving this task undone?*" (For example, you could be scolded by the boss, or could be fired)

5) If the answer is "*YES, I'm not willing to pay the consequences*", then DON'T DO IT. You have decided that the consequences are less serious than the action.

6) If the answer is "*NO*", then DO IT, you have decided that the consequences of not acting are worse than the action.

You may ask yourself. How is this different than *willing* myself to complete a task? The answer is self-awareness. You became aware of your own procrastinating thought patterns and you confronted them. Instead of going into an energy-consuming battle where you forced yourself to do something *despite* not wanting to do it, you changed your emotions and therefore changed your will. You took control not only the situation, but of your own mind. This is a power accomplishment.

Hey, there's an extra bonus for you!

www.personalproductivityproject.com/happinessformula

The fence

To strengthen the ability to say NO, people need to be aware of their own thoughts and the mechanisms that lead them to procrastinate. To make everything easier, it is useful to recognize the typical words we use when we are procrastinating: "*not yet…*", "*I don't feel like it…*", "*wait...*", "*you can do it later…*", with the emotions that accompany them.

The first thing to do is activate an internal "radar" to recognize when you start having thoughts of procrastination. Just focus the radar on the words we have already seen: "*still 5 minutes*", "*I do it another time*" etc. Observing your thoughts, you will learn to recognize the words you use to procrastinate.

The second is to learn to observe one's thoughts in a calm and neutral way, without judging them or reacting emotionally. Many thoughts are automatic, therefore out of our control. No need to fight them or oppose them. It is enough to let them pass without saying anything. You can start with lower mail situations and become familiar with your thought patterns and learn how to deal with them when they are not useful to you.

When you have learned to choose your thoughts, you will be able to build your mental enclosure. Within the enclosure, there are the conscious choices you've decided to follow. Outside there are temptations, thoughts of procrastination, friends who tell us what we want to hear, etc. And the fence is formed by the word NO, which defends like a wall, against misleading temptations and thoughts. You decide what thoughts you are going to let go through the fence.

How to Build Stronger Self-Discipline

How is it that those incredible individuals we often hear about (or sometimes know personally) manage to achieve so much in their life? How do they have the discipline to wake up earlier than everyone else each morning, stick to a strict, nutritious health and fitness regimen and even have time to read several chapters of an inspirational book or listen to a podcast? All before someone else on the opposite end of the spectrum, has even mustered the energy to get out of bed this morning?

How do you start building this kind of self-discipline too? The discipline that is going to take your life to the next phase of success, the way you should have done so long ago if not for procrastination? By following these techniques below:

- **What Do You Want to Change?** Procrastinators often have several habits in their life that they want (and need) to change. Otherwise, they wouldn't be struggling with procrastination to begin with. This is what you need to do right now. Make a list of all the habits that you think are causing you to feel lazy, demotivated, uninspired and procrastinate, and then next to those qualities, make a list of suggestions on how you would go about changing them. Focus on one habit at a time and start working on changing that. Once you're done, move onto the next habit and slowly work your way through the list. Look to other self-disciplined individuals as an example and see which habits you could start to emulate.

- **See Your Failures as Lessons Instead.** Failures along the way are an inevitable part of success. Like a rite of passage. It is something that you must go through to make success and victory that much sweeter and more meaningful. Think of the failures you encounter along the way as lessons which are going to make you stronger, build your resolve and make you a more determined person. What doesn't bring you down, only makes you stronger at the end, and with each triumph, your self-discipline strengthens and grows.

- **Saying No to Temptation.** This is probably going to be the most challenging phase for a lot of people. If temptations were so easy to resist, self-discipline wouldn't be such a struggle to accomplish. Here's where the power of no comes in again. Each time you say no to something that is going to tempt you to procrastinate, your self-discipline grows stronger. Each time you don't give into your desire, you walk away a little bit stronger and a little more disciplined. So keep at it and keep the momentum going, this is how you're going to build your resolve over time.

- **Avoid Last Minute Decisions.** Leaving decisions to the very last second can often result in you making the wrong choices. Which is why you need to now start making it a point to decide on things the moment you know that there is a decision to be made. Putting off and procrastination the decision isn't going to make it go away, it is just going to delay the inevitable. Learning to make decisions as you go trains you to have better self-discipline alone the way too. Like deciding not to be distracted by your phone for the next hour until you get a task done. Or deciding ahead of time you are going to finish this assignment today no matter what and commit to doing it. Deciding on how many emails you're going to respond today. Deciding on how many tasks on your to-do list you're going to complete today. All these little decisions along the way help make you a more efficient, productive person down the road with better control and self-discipline in your life. It minimizes the chaos and hectic-ness that comes with last minute decisions too.

- **Self-Discipline is Part of Being an Adult.** Nobody said being an adult was easy. We have to do things we don't always necessarily like, but you know what? We *survive*. Adults don't wait around for people to tell them what to do and what not to do. The beauty of being an adult is that we have a mind of our own, we take our lives into our own hands and we make choices and decisions for ourselves. As adults, self-discipline is the driving force that keeps us going, pushing us through those uncomfortable moments in life. Remember the waking up each morning and going to work scenario? That's part of being an adult. To train your self-discipline and build its strength, you need to push yourself to do the uncomfortable things you would rather not do instead of waiting for someone else to force you to do it. Taking that proactive step, that initiative to do it on your own is how you build your self-discipline over time.

- **Setting Smaller Goals -** This is a great way to start cultivating a positive mindset and it is also a great way for helping you overcome procrastination. When we set big goals and we fail to accomplish them, then can be a big emotional hit for many. Feeling discouraged, we lose the drive to keep on fighting and moving forward. Eventually, it becomes easier to procrastinate because we simply don't feel like facing another possible failure yet again. You need to set small goals with smaller, more doable steps to accomplish these goals. This is a much better strategy because each time a goal gets smashed, seeing your goal materialize before you will fuel your belief that you can do this. It will make you want to do more, and eventually, your mind starts to believe you are capable of anything. When that happens, procrastination fades away and becomes a problem of the past.

Now that you know how to choose what you want and what you do not want, you also know that everything you do can be the result of a conscious choice and you can free yourself relying on unreliable motivation or unsustainable willpower. At this point in the path you have understood the dynamics of procrastination. Being able to say NO to temptations is now your main weapon, effective and efficient, to overcome procrastination. When you know how to act, you can then begin to take the necessary steps to start organizing your actions.

Part III

CHAPTER 7:

Strategies to Help Stop Procrastinating

How Setting Priorities, Eliminating Distractions, Completing Tasks and Planning

Only now that you know how to overcome procrastination, you can take care of how to better organize your actions, and to do so, you have to do 4 additional steps.

Step 1: How Setting Priorities

Dwight D. Eisenhower was the 34th president of the United States, a five-star general, the founder of NASA and the first Supreme Commander of NATO. It would be an understatement to say that he was a driven man who knew some strategies to success and productivity. Eisenhower had a tool that he used to set his priorities and plan how to use his time efficiently. This is widely known as the Eisenhower Matrix. It looks like this:

The Eisenhower Matrix

	URGENT	NOT URGENT
IMPORTANT	1	2
NOT IMPORTANT	3	4

Everything on Eisenhower's to do list would fall into one of four categories:

1) Urgent and Important

2) Non-urgent and Important

3) Urgent and Unimportant

4) Non-urgent and Unimportant

Things that were Urgent and Important had to be dealt with first. These were things of high importance and value to Eisenhower that needed to be taken care of in a timely matter or that had a pressing deadline.

In daily life this category might include your check engine light being on, a presentation at work two days from now that influences your success at work, or a sick child in need of medical attention. These would be listed in the "Quadrant One." Because these tasks need to be taken care of first. It is the next three categories that often trip people up and have cause them to get bogged down working on things that are of little or no importance to themselves.

In the Second Quadrant, Eisenhower would list things that were Non-urgent and Important. This is the category that needs the most planning and attention. It is the category that will help you focus on what you value the most and help you achieve your long-term goals. In this category, would be things like exercise, time with family, home and vehicle maintenance, further studies, self-improvement, short-term and long-term planning, money management, volunteer work. These are the things focus on self-improvement, relationship strengthening and planning for the future. These are the keys to our sense of fulfillment and success.

There are two main issues that may be preventing you from spending enough time in this category. One is simply not knowing what is important to you or what you want from life. If you decide what you want, you can work towards that goal. If you are unsure, you will end up simply "treading water" and not making progress in any specific direction. The other issue is being so caught up with urgent business (important and unimportant) that you have no time to work on what you value most. It is important to note that if one plans well, life will be less filled with urgent business and life will calm down. For example, good planning and budgeting will prevent the time- and energy-consuming stress of a personal financial crisis. Regular home and vehicle maintenance will help prevent an urgent repair need.

This brings us to the third quadrant, that which is Urgent and Unimportant. These are thrust upon us: a favor, an interruption, a trivial meeting, things that often distract from that which is important. This category must be trimmed wherever possible. Some things can be delegated to others. If a friend asks a favor that you are not suited for, perhaps you can point them in the direction of someone more able to help. Other tasks in this category can be delayed or even eliminated. Learning how to politely decline additional responsibilities that add no value to our lives can help immensely with urgent, unimportant tasks.

The final category of the Eisenhower Matrix is the fourth quadrant, that which is Non-urgent and Unimportant. These tasks simply do not need to be done and can be eliminated or at the very least, pushed to the very bottom of the to-do list. This category would include notorious time wasters and other traps that procrastinators often fall into.

Step 2: Eliminate Distraction

For a procrastinator it is particularly important to eliminate the distractions, for this it is useful to go further into this point. When we eliminate those things that are neither urgent nor important to us, we have more time to focus on the things we want and need to accomplish. I want you to picture a familiar scenario:

You sit down to work at your desk. You glance at the clock and think confidently, "Three hours! I have plenty of time." Then your phone rings, an email "dings" into your inbox and a group text from your kickball team brings in seven new messages. You look at the clock again and suddenly, 3 hours has become 30 minutes. Where did the time go?

It has never been more imperative that we eliminate distractions that rob us of precious time! Specifically, we can be more aware of the time we are wasting on social media or web-browsing. There is even software that helps track and limit time spent online. If it is possible for your situation, you could unplug from the internet entirely while you tackle offline tasks.

As far as the smartphone goes, a small step that just about everyone can benefit from is to turn off notifications. These are almost never helpful and they are a constant time waste. Another way to eliminate distraction is to work with your phone in flight mode, and activate it only when you take a break. You could even your phone off for a time. 'Unplugging' is almost unheard of today, but it is both liberating and helpful in increasing our productivity.

Another form of distraction is clutter and disorganization. It has been shown scientifically that messy environments increase our stress level and affect our ability to focus. If you clean up your work environment, there will be one less thing to worry about when you are trying to focus on what is most important to you.

A last form of distraction is emotional distraction. As we discussed in earlier chapters, our emotions play a big role in our sense of motivation and can be a drain on our energy and ability to focus. There are some people in our lives that seem to bring nothing but drama and negativity. These "emotional vampires" tend to suck all of the positive energy out of our lives. If we can ward off these vampires, we keep our emotional energy in reserve and avoid being bogged down by unnecessary, distracting negativity.

Step 3: Completing Tasks

As a modern society, we have been told that multi-tasking is helpful to get things done. Your internet browser probably has multiple tabs open at any given time and your phone is most likely beside you and interrupting at intervals even as you read this. This has become the norm; it is how we live. But have you ever tried to text and drive at the same time? There is a reason it is dangerous. Doing multiple things at once means that nothing gets done well or efficiently. Learn to do one thing at a time and always carry it to completion. Do not start another task until the first has been completed. You can start by practicing small things like loading the dishwasher, cooking, writing emails, etc. Let the momentum and satisfaction of a task completed carry you onto bigger, more important tasks.

If at first you struggle to stay focused, chose a set timeframe or even set a timer. For example, you can work at a task for 10 minutes, take a break and then continue at the task at 10 minute intervals until the task is completed. As this becomes easier, you can train yourself to focus for longer periods of time.

Step 4: Planning (to Beat Procrastination and Increase Productivity)

Once you have utilized your Eisenhower Matrix to see which are the most urgent and useful tasks for you to focus on, you need to use thus information to make a to-do list for each day. Before you go to bed, write a to-do list for the next day. You can start small and build. Write a basic list of what you need to accomplish the next day. At the end of the day, review your list. If you did not complete a task write down why it wasn't done and reschedule it. Strive to finish everything on your list. As you become more comfortable with the system you can write more detailed lists with specific time goals. (e.g. 10 AM – 11 AM respond to emails, 11 AM –12 PM phone calls, etc.)

Find ways to make your life more efficient. If there are any aspects of your life in which you could save some time, it's about time you started doing it. Saving yourself some time in some areas will leave more time for you to attend to the other, more pressing matters. For example, if you were to invest 2 or 3 hours one day during the weekend to prepare your meals for the rest of the week, you'll save so much time during the rest of the week because you're not busy cooking your dinner or your lunch, which leaves you more time to attend to other matters. Look at all the tasks you have to attend to and see where you can group similar activities together so you can tackle them in one go. Increase your productivity by minimizing the time spent working on activities individually.

Another tip for planning to increase productivity is to think about when you are at you most productive. Are you a night owl or early bird? Different people are productive at different times. Some people feel more motivated in the morning, some feel that way in the evening. If you want to make the most out of your productivity streak, find the times when you feel the most energetic and productive, and choose that time to make the most of your tasks schedule. Once you figure out your best time of day, you can also plan your most important tasks for when you are at your sharpest. If you focus best in the quiet hours after midnight, it isn't such a good idea to attempt a complex task first thing in the morning. Go with what works best for you.

CHAPTER 8:

When Procrastination Is Not the Problem

Other Issues Which *Look* Like Procrastination: Not Knowing Where to Start, Perfectionism, Inner Conflict

It may happen that the typical dynamics of procrastination are not the cause of inaction. These are specific events, outside the context of this book and for this they will be described in a simplistic way, but it is useful to have awareness of it. The first is not knowing where to start, the second is perfectionism and the third is inner conflict.

Not Knowing Where to Start

In this case, instead of choosing instant gratification over a delayed reward, a person delays action because they are overwhelmed by possibilities and does not know how to begin. In this instance, you might continually research options without ever starting towards your goal. It can be extremely overwhelming and stressful when you feel like you're being faced with multiple choices, and you don't have the faintest idea where to begin. When dealing with important, life-changing decisions, it can be even more stressful, especially with the pressure of knowing you have to make the right choice.

Sometimes it is the excess of information that confuses the ideas: especially today that it is so easy to find any information online, it can be difficult to organize and choose which ones are suitable, at a certain moment, for us.

In this case, it is better to simply start and course correct along the way. A simple and effective way to overcome this indecision is to set a deadline and start. It is better to make changes along the way than to waste time waiting for the perfect moment. Small steps are better than no steps at all. You don't always need to have all the answers to everything before you begin. Remember that our old friend motivation often shows up once we've started on the journey. Along the way, dig into that motivation to keep you going, remember why you started in the first place.

Doing something is better than doing nothing at all, and this is something your future self will definitely thank you for. Even if you make mistakes and stumble along the way, hey, at least you reached the end and finished it!

Perfectionism

Another exception to the general procrastination rule is perfectionism. A perfectionist has strong beliefs about how their work or project should look. The problem is that what he seeks, perfection, does not exist in this world. The perfectionist then follows something he cannot get. The perfectionist is frozen by the inability to achieve his own lofty standard. According to some psychologists the antidote is to question analyze your beliefs and replace them with rational ones. If you are a perfectionist unable to start a project, you can question yourself: "do I believe that there is only one right way to do this? Is this a true statement, or are there many possible acceptable ways to complete this task? What other result can be considered acceptable?"

The perfectionist is likely to use all the time available to create a perfect project and to have no more time to make it happen. Imagine what would happen if companies like Apple were to make a product only after creating the perfect project. We probably would never have heard of this company. What all companies commonly do is set a good quality standard for the market, start production and then improve the product.

Perfectionists can set unreachable goals for themselves sometimes, and then it hits them hard if they fail to accomplish those goals because of that high level of expectation they set for themselves. Aiming too high, especially when the expectations are unrealistic, is a surefire way to set yourself up for failure. When you spend far too much time planning for perfection, you come up with all sorts of excuses to procrastinate and delay your plan because it will *never be perfect enough* to be executed in time.

Sometimes you just need to look at things realistically, see the facts in front of you and accept that nothing can ever be as perfect as you want 100% of the time.

Inner conflict

The third case is that of the inner conflict. Each person has a system of internal rules that they on a subconscious level. These rules help them to determine which actions they should take. These rules also shape the perception that they have of themselves. For example, Person A has an image of themselves as someone who is enterprising and successful. Person A would never put themselves in a position as that of a regular employee for example, because it would conflict with the subconscious idea and perception which they have already formed of themselves.

We may not realize it, but every action that we take often passes through the scrutiny of our internal rule system. If the decision agrees with our internal rules, we have no problems executing it. However, if it disagrees, that is when internal conflict happens. What happens though, when an action that is being mulled on agrees with some of the internal rules but conflicts with others? This is yet another scenario of internal conflict taking place. One half (the half which agrees with the rules) wants to execute the action, but the other half (the half which disagrees) hesitates. Internal conflict, is like a tug of war between two teams.

This is what procrastination looks like. An internal conflict which is happening within you. One half of you wants to do it, but the other half is tempted not to. It is useful to reflect and think about our internal dynamics to help us make full use of the Happiness Formula (chapter 6). This formula makes it easier to determine which values are a priority, and which are not.

Conclusion

Think about all the times you have felt stressed and felt disappointed because you know you could have done more. Remind yourself of this feeling, because that is the emotional cost of procrastination. That is what you're looking at for the next several years if you continue to *not* take any action and let procrastination rule the day. The only way your life is going to change is if you *do something to change it*.

It is important for you to be aware of one thing: any action, including that of postponing, is a building block with which you are building your life. The smallest bricks are the easiest to collect, but even with them, when you have many, you can create a grandiose construction. For this reason, the biggest life changes you make can often be in the smallest actions and decisions you make, and it is important not to lose the opportunity to act.

Overcoming procrastination can take some time, but you can divide the journey into many small steps, and each of these steps will make the next one easier. Whenever you find yourself struggling, just look back at these strategies to help steer you back on track again. Because of the knowledge you now have, you're already one step closer towards successfully beating the procrastination habit which is has been following you around for long enough. It is now time for you to shine and live the productive life that you owe it to yourself. Everyone has the potential within them to achieve greatness. Your journey is about to begin.

Made in the USA
Middletown, DE
22 February 2019